A SPIRIT DAUGHTER WORKBOOK

WRITTEN BY
JILL WINTERSTEEN

FOR THE FULL MOON
SATURDAY, JUNE 3RD, 2023
8:42PM PT

SAGITTARIUS FULL MOON

When Sagittarius meets the Full Moon, we feel a need for adventure. Sagittarius carries the energy of the wanderer, teacher, and philosopher. It is also the muse and the truth-seeker. Depicted as the half-man, half-horse with a bow and arrow in hand, this sign is many things. It teaches us that we are many things too. When we remain curious about the many facets of ourselves, we continually expand our consciousness.

SAGITTARIUS FULL MOON

The important piece to remember about Sagittarius's energy is that it is ultimately about truth. And the journey to find that truth is where all the magic happens. As the arrow flies through the air from the hands of the archer, it experiences many currents of reality. These flashes of insight and larger-picture views are more important than where the arrow lands. As you journey through this Full Moon, think of yourself as that arrow. Gather what you need to know without concern about where you will land. Let yourself take twists and turns as needed to experience the winds of change coming toward you. Be open to viewing your reality from a different perceptive and always keep searching for the bigger picture.

This powerful Strawberry Moon teaches us to honor the great quests of our life. Some of these quests may be actual adventures that carry us to far-off places, like climbing Machu Picchu or sailing around the world. Others may be adventures that keep us closer to home, like having a child or starting a company. Some of the greatest adventures of all can take place in the mind as we break through old patterns and climb to a new level of consciousness. While these quests vary greatly in the details, they all take us someplace new in our energy, deliver us undeniable truths, and ask us to confront our greatest fears. As you work with the Full Moon, feel what great quest you are currently on or what is calling you toward it. Sagittarius teaches us to take leaps of faith that help us overcome our fears and assume the best will happen.

Sagittarius is known for its positive vibrations but sees the world as neither positive nor negative. What happens just is, and it's always meant to be. Sagittarius helps us find the silver linings in the most challenging circumstances. It teaches us that life is full of many lessons, and as long as you are learning, you are living. On any adventure, there will be twists and turns. Whether you are climbing a mountain, raising a child, or sitting in silence for tens of days on a meditation retreat, there will be challenges. There will also be moments of insight, gratitude, and hope. There will be dark nights when you feel alone and cold. There will be bright mornings when you exude gratitude for every breath. Adventures of any kind are not supposed to be easy and carefree all of the time. If they were, they would fail to deliver the lessons we need. While we can learn pivotal insights from a path of ease, it's often the more tumultuous ones that deliver the greatest wisdom.

As we begin to appreciate the wisdom gained from some of the harder roads we've walked, it becomes easier to choose new ones. Instead of fearing what could happen, we understand that anything could happen at any time and we will always make the most of it. Sagittarius does not guarantee a happy life full of rainbows and unicorns. It guarantees that when you are willing, you can find the higher meaning of any life experience. You can make a hundred different varieties of lemonade out of lemons if you take the time to learn the recipes. Then you can go on to be the teacher of those recipes and even the philosopher who guides those around them to ultimate truths.

As you work with this Full Moon, remind yourself that it is a journey of truth. Ask yourself what adventures are calling you and what truths they will deliver once you complete them. Then decide if you are ready for those truths right now. If the answer is yes, confront your fears, take a leap, and know that you will make the best-case scenario unfold. Release anything blocking you from taking this leap and step forward into a new adventure. If you need help, ask the Universe for a sign and follow it. Be aware of messages this day and know that they are always leading you on the path of higher consciousness.

SAGITTARIUS MOON X GEMINI SUN

On the Full Moon in Sagittarius, we are also working with the energy of Gemini, where the Sun is located. As the Moon and Sun oppose each other, they reveal the full spectrum of vibrations governed by the Gemini and Sagittarius axis. In this revelation, we can fully view and feel where we align with both the higher and lower frequencies of each of these signs. We all hold the energies of Sagittarius and Gemini within our energetic body, even if these are not strong placements in your natal chart. You carry the energy of all twelve zodiac signs and can align with the higher or lower frequencies of each one at different times. The Sagittarius Full Moon is an opportunity to recognize how you integrate these energies where you may be holding on to lower vibrations Once you are aware of these attachments, you can release them and shift into a higher energy.

Sagittarius and Gemini are two sides of the same coin. Where Gemini focuses on the details, Sagittarius sees the bigger picture. Where Gemini communicates to learn, Sagittarius communicates to teach. Where Gemini searches for duality to understand the world, Sagittarius seeks ultimate truths that provide a higher unification of all energies. Both of these energies are needed at different times to help us learn, evolve, and open our perspectives. When we can learn how to integrate their higher vibrations, we see the details and are able to connect them to understand the greater meaning of any experience. These two signs form the axis of the mind and, in many ways, help us integrate our left, logical brain with our right, creative side. Their integration helps us remain curious, ask questions, and look for answers while knowing that we are really searching for a higher understanding. We also understand how to take these higher philosophies and apply them to daily tasks. Blending the higher vibrations of Sagittarius and Gemini helps us find the magic in the mundane.

To find the higher integration of both energies, we must first look at the pieces. Gemini is the sign of the twins. These two beings communicate with each other to gain information and to find two opposing sides of every situation. Gemini's energy moves quickly to help us scan any experience and find the details within it. This fast-paced nature also allows us to find dualities present. By looking at the extreme sides of any energy, we can gain a greater understanding of the whole picture.

When we align with the opportunities Gemini presents, we become fascinated by the world around us, desiring to know everything we can about its mysteries. We become the observer, which in turn makes us less reactive to our emotions. Gemini's high side allows us to detach from our emotions while remaining present with them. This nonreactive state allows us to continue learning without closing our minds due to fear, misunderstanding, or anxiety. It also allows us to receive messages from the Universe. When we are open to different forms of communication, we open ourselves to receiving signs from the world around us. Gemini's energy can help us receive much-needed information on our paths if we are willing to acknowledge it.

Every energy has a low and a high side. Gemini's low, or shadow, side includes judgment, close-mindedness, and ungrounded energy. When we align with this side, our nervous energy takes over, and we become fearful of the world around us. The mind races from one thought to another, with nothing to center it. We react to our emotions either with anxiety or by numbing ourselves so we feel nothing at all. In this state, we cannot correctly process our feelings, and they wreak havoc behind the scenes. To control the anxiety, we inundate ourselves and the people around us with questions while we look for answers. We ignore intuition and insist that logic is the only way. We may even develop tunnel vision, focusing on only certain aspects of a situation and forgetting the bigger picture.

If you find yourself aligning with the lower frequencies of Gemini on this Full Moon, or at any time, ground yourself through your breath and body. Do some yoga to connect with your physical energy, getting yourself out of your head. Try to feel your emotions, even if they scare you. Rely on the communication Gemini offers to journal, talk to a friend, or even just listen as someone talks to you. Feel your intuition guiding you and trust that all the answers you need in this moment will easily come to you. You do not need to worry about the future or try to control it. You just need to be open to communicating with yourself and the world around you in the present moment.

Sagittarius, much like Gemini, also inspires us to gain information. When we align with this higher vibration, we seek expansion. We search the world for new insights and perspectives. We absorb information at rapid speed and seek to integrate it with what we already know. We also trust that everything will work out how it's meant to, even in the face of adversity. Sagittarius's high-side energy allows us to see life as a perpetual journey of unraveling truths. There is no endpoint, and we can never exhaust the world's knowledge. There are always new truths to learn and new perspectives to incorporate into our own understanding.

The high side of Sagittarius shows us the infinite potential of our consciousness and encourages us to expand it with every opportunity. In this frequency, we become open to receiving new truths and taking leaps of faith. We trust the journey of life and know that even if we stumble, we are still learning. Life becomes an evolving experience where there are no failures, no wrong turns, and no mistakes. There are just new realities to encounter that will expand our consciousness to new levels. With each level, we evolve our energy and broaden our connection with the Universe.

As joyful and wonderful as the energy of Sagittarius is, it too has a low side. Sagittarius, in its shadow side, loses faith. When we align with this vibration, we lose trust in ourselves, our paths, and even the Universe. We question the meaning of our existence and allow ourselves to fall into a downward spiral of questions that even the greatest philosophers cannot answer. Sagittarius, in its lowest state, causes us to experience an existential crisis, preventing us from moving forward in life. We become stuck in an infinite loop of contemplation. We fail to launch into something new and question the point of everything. We question the meaning of our lives and the meaning of everything that has happened to us. We expect disappointment and take a pessimistic view of our journey. Fear-based decisions control us, and we may even start assuming worst-case scenarios, focusing on the negative. Life begins to feel pointless in this vibration.

If you find yourself in this frequency of Sagittarius, take even the smallest step forward into something new. Even if you cannot take a huge leap, find some way to bring new energy into your life. Make a breakthrough in your energy by taking a chance in any direction. Remind yourself of the higher meaning of your life and focus on the positive of a past event, even if it's challenging to find it. Take a broad look at your life in the context of the planet, and see the whole point of it all.

As you recognize some of these energies within yourself, know that it's ok to hold lower energies in your field. We all do at certain times. Becoming aware of them changes everything and opens the doorway for a higher vibration. The Full Moon can teach you how to take great leaps of faith as you overcome fear and find higher meaning. It can then help you take these higher lessons and apply them to all of life. We can't all sit on a mountaintop contemplating life forever. The real journey begins when you are able to take what you've learned on your great quests and apply it to the smaller moments of life. This Full Moon can help you understand how to find grand insights and use them when you're sitting in traffic, changing a diaper, or gaining the courage to speak up in a meeting. Whatever adventure is calling you, now is the time to embrace it.

ASPECTS

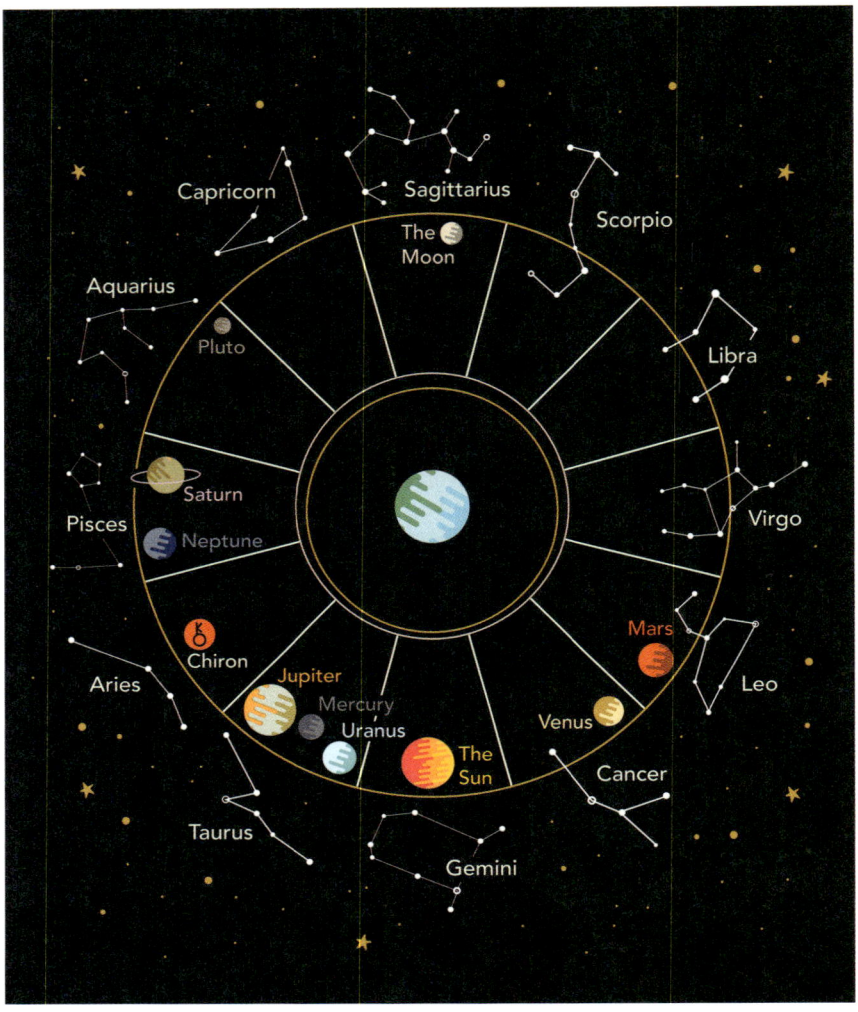

Every Full Moon brings us a myriad of energy to work with in addition to the Sun and Moon. Other planets form aspects with the Full Moon, shifting the vibrations we feel from the event. Aspects are also what make this Sagittarius Full Moon feel different from last year's. Each Full Moon brings us unique energy and even differing themes compared to Moons before.

During the current Sagittarius Strawberry Full Moon, the Moon trines Mars in Leo, adding more fire to this day. Trines occur when cosmic bodies are 120° apart in the sky. They are beneficial aspects and allow the vibrations of each planet to harmonize with the other planet's vibrations. Mars is the planet of passion. It encourages us to find what we love most in the world and pursue it with courage. This planet also teaches us when to fight for what we love and stand our ground like a confident warrior.

ASPECTS

When Mars lands in Leo, we are given extra courage to follow our hearts. This transit helps us take an extra leap into a new adventure aligned with who we really are. Leo helps us face our vulnerabilities and even embrace them as strengths. As Mars transits Leo, let yourself express and pursue your passions. Allow others to see what you love. It's also important to remember the art of non-attachment. This energy is intense and can cause us to hold on to things that are best released. It's a great time to look at why you might be attached to certain things and if this attachment is rooted in your ego or identity. If you find yourself fighting to hold on during this transit, ask yourself why.

Mars in Leo brings enthusiastic energy to the Full Moon. You may feel ready to conquer a new mission or excited about a new path. Align with this energy if you need an extra boost to overcome any fear. Feel your inner warrior and know that you are ready to overcome any obstacles on your path. Lead yourself forward with passion and heart into new territory full of unknown possibilities.

There are a few other aspects to work with today that don't involve the Moon or Sun but still affect the energy of the day. Venus lands in Cancer as it opposes Pluto in Aquarius. Venus is the planet of love and brings us in touch with our hearts. In Cancer, Venus reminds us to take care of our hearts, nourish them, and allow them to lead. Pluto is the ruler of transformation. In Aquarius, it brings its transformation to the collective. Pluto in Aquarius helps us heal and understand what we bring to society this lifetime.

As Venus and Pluto oppose each other this Full Moon, they illuminate issues around the heart. It's a time to feel any wounds in this area and ask if they are holding you back from taking a step forward. This Moon holds the opportunity to find silver linings and higher meaning in your heartache. First, though, you must listen to your heart and ask what it needs. Place any wounds of the heart within the larger picture of your life. You may even be able to place it within the larger picture of your many lifetimes. Become aware of what lessons you've learned from your heartache and how those lessons have helped you find some truth about yourself. What do you know about yourself now because of your heart's journey? Spend some time nourishing yourself, and when you feel ready, ask your heart if it feels brave enough to start anew.

We have another aspect to work with this Full Moon. Jupiter in Taurus sextiles Saturn in Pisces. Jupiter is the ruling planet of Sagittarius. Its energy largely affects the Full Moon. Jupiter in Taurus asks us to slow down and feel our expansion. It asks us to witness our energy unfolding instead of unconsciously moving through life. Jupiter in Taurus brings the opportunity to connect deeply with yourself and feel your ability to create abundance. As Jupiter sextiles or lands 60° away from Saturn, we are asked to look at our commitments.

Over this Full Moon, ask yourself what adventures you are ready to commit to and if these adventures will expand you. Feel your potential calling you even if you need to slow down to hear it. Align with the energy of Jupiter in Taurus to feel your resilience and know that you are always supported by the Universe and yourself. You are your own safety net, so take the leap that is in front of you, remembering that you are always held and nurtured.

JUPITER PLACEMENTS

HOW YOU INTERACT WITH ABUNDANCE

WHERE YOU MAY BE MISSING YOUR POTENTIAL

WHERE YOU HAVE ROOM FOR EXPANSION AND GROWTH

HOW YOU TAKE LEAPS OF FAITH AND ATTRACT LUCK

Just as we all have a Sun and a Moon sign, we also have a Jupiter sign, the place Jupiter was positioned when we were born. In your natal chart, Jupiter shows where you have room for expansion. It also shows how you interact with abundance, leaps of faith, and luck. It can show the place of your full potential and where you may be selling yourself short.

Jupiter is the ruling planet of Sagittarius. On the Full Moon in Sagittarius, Jupiter is also activated and plays a role in how you will experience this Full Moon. By knowing your Jupiter placement, you can pay attention to the part of your personality ruled by Jupiter. These areas are amplified on the Sagittarius Full Moon, and you can understand them more deeply as the Full Moon highlights them. Below is a description of the energy Jupiter brings to your chart and personality determined by its placement in the sky when you were born. You can look up your chart at astro-charts.com.

JUPITER PLACEMENTS

JUPITER IN ARIES: With Jupiter in Aries, you are full of energy and ready for anything. You rise to any challenge, knowing you have the courage, wisdom, and good karma to overcome it. Jupiter in Aries gives you a burst of energy, especially when facing fears and adversity. Feel this part of yourself on this Full Moon to charge forward into unknown territory. Know that you are resilient and can always bounce back from any setback, no matter how deep the wound. You are also quite the trailblazer and tend to have many ideas on what to do next. Your true potential comes when you commit to one path and see it through to completion, allowing it to expand your spirit in the process.

JUPITER IN TAURUS: With Jupiter in Taurus, you expand through simple moments. Your growth requires a firm foundation and stable ground. You thrive with routine and rituals. Your greatest asset is your self-worth, which comes from the inner knowing that you can always rely on yourself. You have the potential to be abundant in any energy, as long as you feel worthy of it. On this Full Moon, allow yourself to expand into unknown territory that feels good to your senses. Allow yourself to be quiet and open. This stillness allow the world to open up for you.

JUPITER IN GEMINI: With Jupiter in Gemini, you expand through knowledge. You have an innate thirst for information, devouring books, articles, and conversations with ease. You also love to share what you've learned with others, often commanding the energy of the room. It's important for you to remember that not everyone shares your enthusiasm for information, but some will. Seek out the people who are most receptive to your energy and consider them partners in your exploratory process. On this Full Moon, people will be more outgoing than usual. Take the opportunity to not only share your ideas but listen to others and let their energy help you expand.

JUPITER IN CANCER: With Jupiter in Cancer, you expand through your home. You may even have good fortune in finding the perfect home to soothe your soul. You grow through quiet time in the right environment and with people who feel supportive. Family is important to you, whether they are your biological family or your soul family. You cherish the people in your life and rely on them to pull you out of your cave when needed or come in to keep you company when the weather isn't right for an outing. On the Full Moon, focus on things that feel like home to expand your energy. You may even find that different places feel like home at different times in your life. Experiment with the meaning of home and know that all definitions expand you.

JUPITER IN LEO: With Jupiter in Leo, you are the star of the show. You expand through open-hearted performances that show your raw vulnerability. You are here to lead, and in a big way, but this leadership must be done with utmost sincerity. To reach your full potential, let people into your inner world, even if it feels scary. Show all sides of yourself and know that when you do, you draw people in even closer. Your audience will appreciate you more and trust your leadership the more you reveal to them. If you are honest with yourself and those around you, the royal kingdom is yours. On this Full Moon, dare to show your heart in some way and notice where you hesitate. Then do the work to release those blocks.

JUPITER PLACEMENTS

JUPITER IN VIRGO: With Jupiter in Virgo, you expand when you know your worth. You are here to be seen for your work, and that work helps everyone. You are a natural healer and often grow by helping others. Your work is first to honor your brilliance and know your self-worth. You carry a great gift, and when you accept this, you can then begin to change the lives of those around you. On the Full Moon, release fear around not being good enough. Take a leap of faith, trusting yourself and what you have to offer.

JUPITER IN LIBRA: With Jupiter in Libra, you expand through art and the people to share it with. You excel at anything that asks you to harmonize colors, textures, or vibrations. You seek out beauty and need people around you who appreciate the world's colors just as much as you do. It's important for you to enjoy the beauty of a sunset, the colors of a flower, or the notes of a beautiful piece of music. These things expand you and help you feel your center. From here, you can move forward with ease and grace into any area that calls you. On the Full Moon, broaden your horizons with something you find beautiful.

JUPITER PLACEMENTS

JUPITER IN SCORPIO: With Jupiter in Scorpio, you expand by diving deep into the waters of life. Anything that probes at the underpinnings of consciousness piques your interest. You may find yourself a student of shamanism, tarot, astrology, or psychology. These things help you find your potential and raise your vibration. You also seem to find the brighter side of even the darkest topics, adding a little lightness into the conversation when it begins to feel heavy. Your sense of humor helps any situation, and you know how to wield it with kindness and compassion. On the Full Moon, honor your own sacredness, feeling your power. Let the light of the Moon remind you that you are here to grow, evolve, and expand.

JUPITER IN SAGITTARIUS: With Jupiter in Sagittarius, luck is on your side. Jupiter is the planetary ruler of Sagittarius and is at home in this sign. You expand through adventure and experiences that help you evolve. You are here to learn, explore, and make mistakes. Everything on your path, though, is there to help you gain wisdom and understand the Universe at its very core. As long as you stay focused on your soul's growth, you can do no wrong. There are no wrong turns or misfortunes, only opportunities to discover something about yourself or the world. On this Full Moon, release any fear and know that you have the support of the Universe in any leap you take. So jump.

JUPITER IN CAPRICORN: With Jupiter in Capricorn, you expand through focus and attention. Your eyes are always on the prize, and this habit helps shape your greatness. You can get things done that others cannot, and you excel at challenging tasks. In fact, the more complex the task, the more enjoyable it becomes. To reach your full potential, add balance and fun into your life. Take time to enjoy nature, people, and self-care rituals. All of these things are part of your life's work. You may also find that when you take a break from your work, the answers you are seeking appear and you do not need to overthink them. On the Full Moon, decide on what risk you are ready to take in your life. It may be calculated, but it's time to take a chance for a life you love.

JUPITER IN AQUARIUS: With Jupiter in Aquarius, you expand through unique experiences that teach you about yourself. You are different from most and have unconventional ideas about the world. You can reach your full potential by embracing these ideas and sharing them with the world. You may even find yourself starting a business that helps the world innovate with new technology and progressive ideas. You are a visionary, and when you embrace this aspect of yourself, you grow—and the world grows with you. On the Full Moon, become aware of any fear holding you back from your full potential. Release anything that blocks you from being you.

JUPITER IN PISCES: With Jupiter in Pisces, you expand through spirituality and connecting with your divine wisdom. You are a child of the Universe. To reach your full potential, honor your dreams, visions, and capacity to heal. Help others through acts of service that inspire you. Always put your evolution first and know that you are here to understand things that will be with you through many lifetimes. Embrace your intuition each day and know that it is your guide to some of your most incredible experiences. On the Full Moon, take care of your energy. Cleanse your energetic field and commit to practices that help you honor your magic without fear.

SAGITTARIUS LUNAR FLOW

Sagittarius rules the hips and thighs. She also rules the hip flexors, including the psoas, a muscle that runs from the mid-spine to the front of the hips. It is primarily responsible for helping us walk. Energetically, the psoas controls the flight-or-fight response. It allows us to either curl up in a ball or charge forward. It contracts when we are feeling fear. Often, fear stagnates here, affecting our ability to change.

During a Sagittarius Full Moon, we want to open the hips and psoas so we are free to walk into new territory, both mentally and physically. Through opening this area, we release fear and permit ourselves to step into our destiny.

SUN SALUTATION WITH LUNGE: 3 ROUNDS

Stand at the top of your mat. Inhale, stretch your arms overhead > Exhale, fold forward > Inhale, lengthen out your back > Exhale, step your right foot back, lower your knee to the ground > Inhale, lift your arms and torso up into a low lunge > Exhale, step back to Plank Pose, and lower > Inhale, reach your chest up for Cobra Pose, legs on the ground > Exhale, Downward Dog Pose. Stay here for 5 breaths and feel your entire body expand. On the exhale, step your right foot forward, lower your back knee to the ground > Inhale, reach your arms and torso to the sky > Exhale, lower your arms, and step to the top of the mat > Inhale, lengthen through your spine > Exhale, fold forward > Inhale, come all the way up to standing, reaching arms overhead > Exhale, hands to your heart. Pause for a moment and feel yourself centered throughout your body. On your third round, remain in Downward Dog and breathe for 5 breaths.

CRESCENT LUNGE WITH TWIST

From Downward Dog, step your left foot forward into a Lunge Pose. Your back heel will lift from the ground and your leg will stay straight. Bend deeply into your front knee as you tilt your tailbone toward the ground. Reach your arms toward the sky and send your breath into your hips. After 5 breaths, reach your right arm forward and left arm back, twisting to the left. Breathe here for 5 breaths, then place your right hand down, 12 inches from your left foot, and reach your left arm up for a deeper twist. Release both hands to the ground and step back into a vinyasa or Downward Dog. Repeat on the right side.

WARRIOR 2 > REVERSE WARRIOR > EXTENDED WARRIOR (BOTH SIDES)

From Downward Dog, step your left foot forward for Warrior 2. Spin your back foot flat on the ground at a 45-degree angle inward and rotate your torso to the right side of the mat, reaching your arms to either side. Bend your front knee, pressing it out to the left.

Take 5 breaths here, opening up your pelvis and grounding down through your legs. After 5 breaths, rotate your left palm to the sky and arch your back for Reverse Warrior. Reach your left arm in line with your ear and stretch open the left side of your body. Spend 5 breaths here, then lift your torso. Place your left elbow on your left knee for Extended Warrior. Reach your right arm overhead in line with your ear. Spend 5 breaths here, then place your hands back to the ground, stepping back into a vinyasa or Downward Dog for 5 breaths before switching sides.

TRIANGLE > HALF MOON > CHAPASANA

From Downward Dog, step your left foot forward. Angle your back foot at 45 degrees and line up your arch with your front heel. Lift your torso up and straighten your front leg. Reach your arms out to either side and hinge forward into Triangle Pose. Place your left hand on the ground on the outside of your left foot or on your shin, then rotate your torso to the right. Stretch and reach upward through your right arm, feeling one long line of energy from fingertip to fingertip. Stay here for 5 breaths, then place your left hand about 12 inches in front of your left foot, bending your front knee. Launch forward into Half Moon Pose, lifting your back leg and pressing through that heel. Your toes will be facing to the right. Find your balance here, then slowly begin to bend your right leg and catch hold of the top of your foot for chapasana. Try to keep your leg parallel to the ground as you open the front of your hip by kicking your foot into your hand. Remain here for 5 breaths, then slowly release to Downward Dog, switching sides.

LIZARD POSE > HALF SPLITS POSE

From Downward Dog, step your left foot outside your left hand. Lower your back knee and sink your hips forward. Feel the front of your right thigh opening as you breathe. If you'd like to go deeper, you can lower to your elbows. After 5 breaths, bring your front foot back in line with your front hip. Straighten that leg out for Half Splits Pose. Have your hips directly over your back knee and fold forward over your straight leg. Use blocks under your hands if you need to. Keep your back as straight as possible as you fold. After 5 breaths, return to Downward Dog and switch sides.

PIGEON POSE

Return to Downward Dog through a vinyasa or by stepping back. Then take your left knee to your left wrist for Pigeon Pose. Go easy on your knee. If you feel any pain, do Thread the Needle Pose, a Pigeon modification. Carefully lay down your left leg and stretch your right leg back. Before folding, press up through your hands and arch your back a bit, stretching through the front of your body. On exhale, fold forward over your leg and remain here for 10 breaths. On each inhale, send your breath into your hips, encouraging them to open. On exhale, release a bit more. After 10 breaths, slowly switch sides.

SAVASANA

Release onto the floor, lying with your palms up and eyes closed. Feel your body alive with fresh energy circulating freely through it.

SAGITTARIUS MEDITATION

The Sagittarius Full Moon is a powerful time to face and transform fears. Fear has a way of living in our bodies. While it is often at the forefront of our minds, it also can subconsciously change our perceptions and behavior. We can hold fear in different areas of the physical, energetic, and emotional body. Fear, though, always has something to teach us. It can bring us wisdom and help us understand ourselves on a deeper level. It can shed light on blocks and obstacles that prevent us from manifesting our dreams.

When we embrace fear with an open mind, we can understand it. In that understanding, we can take away any power it has over us. Fear may always come to pay us a visit, but we do not have to let it change our course of action or deter our plans in any way. We simply need to listen to it, acknowledge it, and move it out of our bodies. Through facing our fears, we begin to control them and life's course.

The following guided meditation is meant to help you understand your fears and shift them out of your body, making room for your inspiration and courage to blossom.

TALKING WITH YOUR FEARS

The first step in transforming fears is to understand them. Your fear has something to say and wants to be heard. The best thing you can do is listen to it with an open mind. Once your fears are heard, they become less demanding. They are more easily moved away from you as they quiet down, knowing they have expressed their concerns.

Begin in a seated position with your spine upright, eyes closed, and hands placed lightly in your lap. Observe your breath, watching the inhale and exhale. Place all of your focus on feeling your breath in this moment as it enters and leaves your body. Know that you can always place your focus here to calm yourself down and center your energy.

Feel if any fear is living in your body. Observe any tightness or feelings of restlessness in your physical form. Breathe into them and allow them open. Then ask yourself, What fears am I feeling today? Allow your fears to rise up by staying centered on your breath and grounded in your body. As your fears emerge, stay open to them. Become increasingly aware if you are tightening areas of your body and send your breath to them. Attempt to remain open in your physical form even as fears swirl around in your mind.

Choose one fear to focus on. Ask this fear, What do you want to teach me? What are your concerns? What do you think you see that I am blind to? What is your worst-case scenario? Be open to these answers both in your body and in your mind. Stay centered on your breath for a few moments as your fear talks to you. As it speaks, be curious about what your fear wants to teach you.

After you've heard your fear, ask another set of questions. Ask your fear, What will it take for you to trust the process of our life? What will it take for you to feel supported and at ease in our journey? How can I help you surrender to what you can't control? Once again, focus on your breath and give space for your fears to answer.

Slowly open your eyes, then take your pen and write down the answers to the second set of questions, letting them develop even more as you write them onto the paper. Focus on trust and surrender here, and ask your fear once again how it can move toward these vibrations. After you finish writing, return to your seated position with your eyes closed, and focus on your inhale and exhale. Stay here for a few moments, grounding your energy. Then let your nervous system settle as you process your answers.

Feel more at ease in your body and in control of your life. If your fears continue to pop up , sit down and have a conversation with them. Allow them to be heard, then move them toward trust in your life and your path.

SAGITTARIUS CIRCLE SET-UP

On this Full Moon, we are working with the elements of Fire from Sagittarius and Air from Gemini. Air stokes the flames of Fire, allowing these two elements to feed off of each other and combine their energy. Air inspires us, helping us shift and change. Fire helps us burn away anything we no longer want in our lives. This Full Moon is about movement and change. Feel into this energy when creating your space. Make sure there is good airflow and plenty of room for movement if needed. Also, choose a space that feels grounded and connected to Mother Earth. Fire needs an anchor to keep from blowing out of control. You can practice your rituals outside, close to the ground. Or you can choose a space that contains the Wood element. If these are not available to you, place plants and crystals in your circle to bring the Earth inside. You can practice alone or in a community; it's entirely up to you. Sagittarius is a very social sign, so you may be called to practice with others. If this is the case, gather with people who make you feel safe and encourage you to expand into your potential.

Incorporate the rest of the elements into your circle, along with Earth. If possible, build a fire outside, which you can use later for releasing energy. You can also light candles in your space. For Air, incorporate auric sprays, feathers to fan smudge sticks, and even wind chimes to hear the air moving around you. Place crystals in the middle of the circle and around the perimeter. Crystals that align with the energy of Sagittarius are Turquoise, Red Jasper, and Aventurine. These crystals will bring you serendipity and give you the confidence to make a big leap forward. Crystals for Gemini are Agate, Apophyllite, and Chrysocolla. These crystals will help you communicate with your higher Self and become your own teacher. You can also incorporate flowers of both Sagittarius and Gemini into your space, including narcissus, carnations, ranunculus, and daffodils to represent the Earth element. Bring in the element of Water through a room diffuser, a vase, or a metal bowl containing water. Gather all of your supplies and build your circle.

TURQUOISE   RED JASPER   AVENTURINE

AGATE   APOPHYLLITE   CHRYSOCOLLA

Create an outline with your objects, anchoring the four directions—north, south, east, and west—with either a crystal or candle. If you are creating an altar, set it up in the westerly part of the circle, as this direction helps energies release. An altar can contain objects that help infuse wisdom into your space. It can hold crystals, flowers, letters of intentions, and pictures of loved ones or spirit guides. Altars can anchor the energy of a space and give a focal point as you practice. Crystal grids can also anchor the energy and project it outward through its formation. If setting up a crystal grid, have it in the center of the circle, choosing a generator or tower crystal for the center.

SAGITTARIUS CIRCLE SET-UP

Once you've set the perimeter, cleanse the area with a dried herb. Juniper is a wonderful cleansing herb that also provides protection. Begin cleansing at the easterly point, moving to the south, west, north, then back to the east. Imagine a wh te light encasing the circle, protecting it from any external energies. Before any guests enter, cleanse each one of them and then yourself, wafting the smoke around the entire body, including the soles of the feet. Once you have all entered the circle, pause for a moment to let the energy settle before you begin.

Follow your intuitive guidance when leading a circle. Begin with each member introducing themself. Talk about the astrological energy of the day and how it is affecting each one of you. Share and learn from each other about your unique experiences with the Full Moon's energy. Give plenty of space for each person to speak. Follow your conversation with the meditation practice in this book to calm the mind. You can then explore the rest of the practices. Do them alone, but share as much or as little as you want with the rest of the group. Go over the questions and continue to learn from each other's perspectives.

After you've completed the practices, take three pieces of paper. On one, write something you are releasing this Full Moon. On the second, write an intention you are calling in through the element of Air. On the third, write what you are grateful for tonight. Gather all the releasing notes and either burn them (safely) or rip them to shreds. Gather the intention notes and place them under a crystal in the most easterly corner of your home. Leave them there for a week. For the gratitude notes, pass yours to the person on the left, who passes theirs to the person on their left, and so on; everyone will take their neighbor's home. Sharing in others' gratitude is a beautiful way to merge our energy with the collective's. If you are practicing alone, place your gratitude note somewhere you can see it every day. End the circle by giving thanks to everyone who attended, including yourself, and to yourself for showing up.

CARD READING

1 — What energy will help me realize and confront my fears?

+

CARD PULLED:

2 — What energy will help me step out of my comfort zone and into my potential?

+

CARD PULLED:

3 — What energy will help me understand the higher meaning of everything that occurs in my life?

+

CARD PULLED:

Reading Cards is a beautiful way to access your intuition and tap into your, and the Universe's, higher wisdom. Anyone can pull cards, as long as you are willing to receive the information they provide. You need no prior experience, or training, just an open and clear mind.

You may use any cards you like for this practice, including but not limited to: Tarot Cards, Animal Medicine Cards, Oracle Cards or any Affirmation Cards. You also can pull cards from a few decks to gain different perspectives. If you are new to card pulling, try to ask only one deck the same question, as asking different decks the same question can become quite confusing. Below are some general guidelines on how to pull cards. Please improvise as needed and above anything else, listen to your intuition.

CLEAR YOUR MIND

A settled, grounded mind is essential for pulling cards. The last thing you want is random thoughts running around when you are trying to receive clear answers from yourself. Practice the breath work and meditation in this workbook to prepare and settle your mind. You may also clear your mind using sound frequencies through singing bowls. These can either be crystal or metal bowls. Play the bowl, or bowls, for about 3-5 minutes to help rid your mind of external noise as you focus on the harmony of the sound.

CARD READING

PICK YOUR DECK

There are many different decks out there. You can choose as many as you like. Know, though, that they each provide you a different energy or medicine. Tarot Carcs are the most popular and should be used carefully. Although very useful, Taro: cards can give the wrong impression if you interpret them harshly. Animal Medicine cards offer different types of messages from the animal realm which can help align with the spirit of nature. These cards give you the medicine you need to apply to your situation or question. Affirmation cards provide you with guidance in the form of words or phrases. When reading these cards, it is best to meditate on what the affirmation means for you. It is also helpful to repeat the affirmation a few times and see how it makes you feel. There are many other cards you can experiment with, like Goddess Cards, Angel Cards, and so on. The important thing to remember with any card is that they each have different angles and sides. There are cften a few interpretations of the same card.

SHUFFLE

Shuffle the cards the easiest way for you. Some cards are smaller and can be shuffled like a regular deck of playing cards, while others with take some effort. If all else fails, spread them out on the floor in front of you then regather them. Keep a clear mind while shuffling. You can also repeat " I am open to receiving guidance and intuition." Refrain from asking your questions until the next step.

SAGITTARIUS CARD QUESTIONS

You are free to ask the deck any questions you need answers to on this Full Moon. The following questions are meant to help you harness the energy of Sagittarius through the cards to clarify some of these energies in your mind. This is a three-part card reading, where you'll ask the deck three questions. Before beginning, spread your freshly shuffled cards in a wide arc in front of you. Use your left middle finger to choose the card, first waving your hand slowly over the cards. You'll feel a magnetic pull, or slight tingle, in your fingertip when you hover over the right card. Chose one card at a time, taking a moment to breathe in between questions. Keep the cards flipped over until you pull all three.

What energy will help me realize and confront my fears?

What energy will help me step out of my comfort zone and into my potential?

What energy will help me understand the higher meaning of everything that occurs in my life?

TAKE THEM IN

Once you have your cards, flip them over. Before looking up their meaning, sit with them for a moment and allow them to speak to you. Intuit your own meaning and interpretation of the card. What is the card trying to tell you? What are you trying to tell yourself? After a few moments with the cards, look up their meaning. Sit with that information, merging it with your intuitive meaning of the cards.

As with everything, enjoy this process. Do not worry if you are doing it right or wrong. Just follow your intuition, and trust the journey. Accept the cards you are dealt and use their energy wisely to help guide you when you need it the most.

Buy the plane ticket
Quit the job
Accept the date
Start the company
Write the book
Sign up for the class
Make the call
Plan the trip
Wander into the unknown
Open your heart

Take the leap

- spirit daughter

SAGITTARIUS PRACTICES

The Sagittarius Full Moon is a time to feel the bigger picture of our lives. As we do this, we begin to understand the many adventures of our lives and how they all add up to something greater than each individual part. This Full Moon has the potential to help us understand why we've experienced certain things when we did and what lessons can be found in each event. It also can help us embrace new adventures and overcome any fear around pursuing them.

As we work with this Full Moon, we are also working with Gemini's energy. Gemini helps us reframe our life, including events of the past. It can help us find a new perspective of the same situation so we can find the lesson, see the higher meaning, and even release any trauma it may have caused. This Full Moon can help us heal old pain so that we can find the truth of the situation and evolve to a new level of consciousness. As we heal, we release energetic attachments to the past and can embrace new quests without fear or hesitation.

1. What are some of your greatest life adventures?

_____

_____

_____

_____

_____

_____

_____

_____

_____

_____

_____

_____

_____

_____

_____

_____

_____

_____

SAGITTARIUS PRACTICES

2. What have they taught you about yourself?

_____

_____

_____

_____

_____

_____

_____

_____

_____

_____

_____

_____

_____

3. What pain or heartache has come out of any adventure?
   How has it prevented you from welcoming new journeys?

_____

_____

_____

_____

_____

_____

_____

_____

_____

_____

_____

_____

SAGITTARIUS PRACTICES

_____

_____

_____

_____

_____

_____

_____

Often, when we have experienced something negative, we naturally want to avoid that circumstance again. While this process can be advantageous in certain situations, it can also prevent you from enjoying life to your fullest potential. You may hold back your energy or limit yourself in some way because you are scared of experiencing the same negative event again.

When we have endured some kind of trauma, of body or mind, we assume that what was the past will also be the future. We expect and assume the same situation to unfold because that's what we know to be true. We need to consciously teach ourselves that what we think will happen is only a thought. It's not the truth, and we really have no way of knowing what will happen. That alone, though, can be scary until we reassure ourselves that we can find the higher meaning and rely on ourselves no matter what the situation turns out to be.

4. How can you reframe past pain and find the higher meaning in its existence?

_____

_____

_____

_____

_____

_____

_____

_____

_____

SAGITTARIUS PRACTICES

5. How have you shown up for yourself in times of turmoil and seen your strength?

_____

_____

_____

_____

_____

_____

_____

_____

_____

_____

Think about a new adventure that is calling you during this time. This adventure can be anything, including taking a trip, getting married, buying a house, or moving to a new city. Or it can be an inward quest of self-growth and inquiry. Now, think about what leap of faith you need to make to pursue this adventure.

6. How do you feel?

_____

_____

_____

_____

_____

_____

_____

_____

_____

_____

SAGITTARIUS PRACTICES

Is there any fear coming up? What is the fear telling you? Is it valid?

_____

_____

_____

_____

_____

_____

_____

_____

_____

Experiencing fear is a natural part of being human. In some cases, fear serves us very well and keeps us safe from harm. But fear that has no real purpose can block our growth and enjoyment of life. Fear can prevent us from experiencing all that life has to offer. It can keep us trapped in a web of perceived threats when, in reality, we are safe. As you work the Full Moon, make a commitment to overcome the fears blocking you from new experiences.

Remember that we are here to experience life, and not all of those experiences will be pleasant, but plenty will be. Whether they are pleasant or not, though, isn't the point. The point is that the more experiences we have, the more we grow and learn. Our energy does not want to remain stagnant. It wants to shift, and when we transform through experiences, we feel fulfilled on a soul level.

7. Who would you be without your fear?

_____

_____

_____

_____

_____

_____

_____

SAGITTARIUS PRACTICES

8. How do you feel about experiences that don't go as planned? Can you trust that they are part of the bigger picture of your life and energy even if you don't like them?

SAGITTARIUS PRACTICES

As you work with different adventures and experiences in your life, you'll find different lessons. The Sagittarius Full Moon teaches us to find our truths. These may be different from your friend's truths or your parent's, or your partner's. Our truths are unique to us. We may be able to teach them to others, but first, we have to integrate them into our consciousness. When truths are thoroughly integrated, we are able to apply them to any situation that needs them. For instance, if you learn something about yourself while sitting in silence during a ten-day meditation retreat, can you apply that truth to when you are suddenly fired and you have to embark on a new career adventure? Sagittarius teaches us to embrace adventures, find truths, then apply those truths to new experiences. Challenge yourself to connect the dots of your life on this Full Moon and feel your energy integrate in new ways.

9. What are some truths you have learned about yourself through your life experiences?

_____

_____

_____

_____

_____

_____

_____

_____

_____

_____

_____

_____

_____

_____

_____

_____

_____

_____

_____

SAGITTARIUS PRACTICES

10. What are some truths you've learned about life through your experiences?

_____

_____

_____

_____

_____

_____

_____

_____

_____

_____

_____

_____

_____

_____

_____

_____

_____

_____

_____

_____

_____

_____

_____

_____

_____

SAGITTARIUS PRACTICES

11. What other situations can you apply these truths to in order to find the higher meaning in all experiences?

_____

_____

_____

_____

_____

_____

_____

_____

_____

_____

_____

_____

_____

_____

_____

_____

_____

_____

_____

_____

_____

_____

_____

_____

_____

LAST QUARTER: IN PISCES

JUNE 10TH

The Last Quarter is the final phase of the lunar cycle. The energy of this Pisces Moon is here to bring closure to any in-progress releases that started on the Full Moon. This is another chance to cleanse ourselves of anything that is taking up space in our psychic bodies so that we can create room for our dreams to materialize. At this time, any inhibiting self-talk, habits, and fears can be cast away. We often harbor these frequencies in our internal systems to cope with pain and trauma, but when they start to feel more like resistance than protection, we are ready to shed these layers. The Last Quarter Moon can be very healing, and with Pisces energy coming around for the second time in one Sun Season, there is double the amount of restorative power to support you through the process.

Pisces is the healer of the zodiac. Much like the ocean that rules it, the sign carries an ability to be both fierce and graceful, expansive and yet embracing. If you align with this theme and trust that you can release your burdens into its vast waters, you will also be held by these waters. You are divinely supported, even when you cannot see a clear path ahead. Pisces creates a gentle, compassionate space where we can sit with our experiences and recognize that whatever we are currently going through is temporary. Just like the changing tide, nothing in life is constant. So instead of ruminating on our emotions, can we practice simply observing and learning from them?

This is a time to trust in the flow of your life. And when you are not in flow, try to name what is weighing you down. While the familiar may be comforting, it may also hinder your ability to experience a greater trust in yourself and the Universe. What if a new level of joy lies on the other side of your comfort zone? When we let go, we open up a multitude of possibilities for something better to enter our lives.

Harness the Piscean energy of this Last Quarter Moon by being present with water. If you live near a body of water, it would be beneficial to spend time in or around it. A bath can also achieve the desired effects. As you find yourself in this water, surrender to its magical qualities and let it cleanse you of any lingering clutter that was not released on the Full Moon. As the energetic debris dissolves into the water, be at peace knowing that you will be intentionally filling this space again during the next New Moon.

When the moment feels right, take out your journal. Visualizing and embodying the properties of water, write "I feel" at the top of the page. Allow the rest to pour out of you in a stream of consciousness and decline the urge to censor or judge your expression. Give yourself the space to process things you may not have fully realized until this moment. When you are finished, do not rush on to another task. Sit in this moment and focus on your breath, moving your energy through your body and feeling your full potential.

What are you willing to let go this
Last Quarter Moon to allow yourself to
receive new energy?

AFFIRMATIONS

Take a moment and envision taking a leap of faith. What what-ifs or worst-case scenarios come up? What fears come up for you when imagining the unknown?

Write three to five affirmations that counter these what-ifs. You can write positive what-if statements that assume the best will happen, like "What if everything works out?" Or you can write "I am" statements that remind you of your strength and ability to persevere in any situation.

HAPPY
FULL MOON!

Thank you to everyone who supported and purchased this workbook.

Special Thanks to Rebecca Reitz (rebeccareitz.com, @becca_reitz) for her beautiful artwork on the cover & pages 2, 4, 8, 16, 30.

For a monthly subscription contact hello@spiritdaughter.com or visit www.spiritdaughter.com.

Disclaimer: The exercises and yoga sequences in this book are physical activities that should be performed carefully to avoid injury. You agree to accept all risks and release Spirit Daughter and any guest instructors from any and all liabilities. Please take care and enjoy.

Follow along our journey on IG:
@spiritdaughter

We always love seeing your photos & hearing about your experiences with the workbooks! Tag us to be featured on our community page:
@spiritdaughtercollective